The Five Star Program®

A Step-by-Step Teacher's Guide
to Innovative Classroom Strategies
that Awaken Students'
Unique Potential

by
Mariola Strahlberg, M.S., LAc

SHINING MOUNTAIN PRESS
NEW YORK

Brain Gym PACE® material used with permission of the Educational Kinesiology Foundation
Works of Paul Dennison, Ph.D., quoted with permission
Frère Jacques: Melody attributed to Jean-Philippe Rameau / Public Domain
Book, cover, and Five Star Program® flow chart by Wyndjammr Design, *www.wyndjammrdesign.com*
Five Star Program® logo © Daniel Levin, *www.disgustingisgood.com*

Images:
    Photos, pages 10-11, 16, 19-22, 24, 35-36, 45-47, 51 (top)
        © Clyde Hamilton, *imagesphotographyonline.com*
    Photo, page 15, © Dollar Photo Club / locoleal
    Photo, page 27, © Dollar Photo Club / Petro Feketa
    Photo, page 28, © AdobeStock / Khorzhevska
    Photo, page 29, Happy Dayna, author's private collection
    Photo, page 38, © Dollar Photo Club / VTT Studio
    Photos, page 33 and 51 (bottom), © Dollar Photo Club / jovannig
    Leaf illustration, Dollar Photo Club / vladvm50
    Steps illustration, page 22, Dollar Photo Club / shark192009
    Thank you notes on page 52 courtesy of students in grades 4 and 5 at Viola Elementary School,
        Suffern, NY.
    Brain Gym® PACE poster, page 16, and PACE steps photo, page 22, © 2015 by Mariola Strahlberg

Teenage models:
    Abimaelle Belizaire and Andrew Murphy, teen volunteers at the Homework Help program in the
    Finkelstein Library in Spring Valley, NY (2014-2015 school year)
Young models:
    East Ramapo school children at the Homework Help program in the Finkelstein Library in Spring
    Valley, NY (2014-2015 school year)

The procedures and techniques described in this book are solely for informational and educational use, and are not intended to diagnose nor should be construed as a health guide or a manual for self-treatment. Before beginning any exercise program, it is always advisable to check with your professional healthcare providers.

Strahlberg, Mariola
    The Five Star Program®: A Step-by-Step Teacher's Guide to Innovative Classroom Strategies that
    Awaken Students' Unique Potential
    1. Mind and Body - Children 2. Movement Education 3. Teaching Innovations 4. Self-directed
    learning 5. Joy of teaching and learning

Library of Congress Control Number: 2015920973
[Shining Mountain Press] [Chestnut Ridge, New York]
ISBN/EAN13: 0692540596 / 978-0692540596

First Edition

Dedication

This book is dedicated to all the young people who:

- Move when they are supposed to sit still
- Talk when they are supposed to be quiet
- Daydream when they are supposed to pay attention
- "Ignore" instructions when they are given directions
- Have too much energy
- Have too little energy
- Do not do well in reading, math, spelling, reciting, singing, music, or sports

and to all the teachers and educators who:

- Find it difficult to manage their classes with ever increasing numbers of students with individual needs
- Run out of tools to help the students
- Worry that they are not able to reach some of their students
- Are losing their passion for teaching and caring.

Children are not the people of tomorrow, but people today. They are entitled to be taken seriously. They have a right to be treated by adults with tenderness and respect, as equals. They should be allowed to grow into whoever they were meant to be—the unknown person inside each of them is the hope for the future.

—Janusz Korczak (1879-1942)

Free the child's potential, and you will transform him into the world.

—Maria Montessori (1870-1952)

Receive the children in reverence, educate them in love, and send them forth in freedom.

—Rudolf Steiner (1861-1925)

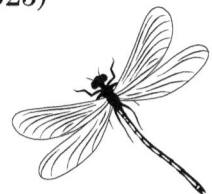

Table of Contents

Level 1 • Part Three

Acknowledgements

There is always somebody to thank when you embark on the journey of writing a book.

In this particular case, my thanks go to all the young people who experienced the Five Star Program® during private sessions, in their classrooms, in after school programs or at camps. They loved it, asked for it, and in a short time wanted to teach it to others. It is for them that this book was written. Many thanks also go to the many parents and teachers who participated in the program and used it effectively not only with the young people in their care, but also for themselves. My hat goes off to you.

The Five Star Program® uses PACE, four movements from Dr. Paul Dennison's Brain Gym®. My thanks go to him for his ability to apply various methods, i.e., Touch for Health, to create a simple system which children learn to love and which teachers and parents find helpful and easy to use.

This book, although written by me, a few months ago was not in the form you are seeing it today. It has come to life thanks to incredible editing by Ronnie Eisen and Debra DeEntremont, designing and producing by Julie Schwartz, and designing of the beautiful logo by Daniel Levin. Thanks also to photographer Clyde Hamilton for the stunning photographs, and to student models Abimaelle Belizaire, Andrew Murphy and East Ramapo school children from the Homework Help program at the Finkelstein Library in Spring Valley, New York, during the 2014-2015 school year.

Big thank you to my volunteers over the years: Janet and Michael Grossman, Dina Grinshpun, Linda Lemery, Lauren Alleva, Ivette Lenard and Delia Tolz for believing in the program and bringing it to the kids. Special thank you to Elisa Ocello for using the initial program for herself and her children and creating initial literature for it.

The Five Star Program® works when it is done alone or in a group, and can be done at any age with minor modifications for those under age five and those who are not in good physical health.

May this book bring a smile to your face, and may you experience many happy, successful moments with your students sharing with them a program that helps them realize their unique capabilities.

Thank you all,

Mariola

THE FIVE STAR PROGRAM®

Introduction: Young People as Leaders in Their Own Learning Process and You, Their Teachers, as Their Guides

Over the years I have studied and experienced many different educational models and two that impressed me the most were Janusz Korczak's humanistic approach of dialogue education and the educational approach of Rudolf Steiner's Waldorf schools. [1] Korczak believed that young people know what they need, want to do better, and as long as they are being heard and appreciated, choose to feel responsible and strive to reach their potential. His action research approach encouraged teachers to first observe themselves and then observe their students. He once said: *"In all cases, I help all who suffer morally. I create conditions for them to heal: lots of light and warmth, freedom and opportunities. I believe that they themselves will want to get better. They will go through their own inner struggles; they will experience their own disappointments and failures. Let them try again and again. Let them look for their own ways. Let them feel joy through single and small victories."* [2]

This book is for those adults who have a passion to help young people reach for the stars. There are some young people for whom school is easy, fun and rewarding. Taking tests and doing homework works well for them and they have lots of free time to enjoy life. There are, however, many other young people who do not like school, have difficulty sitting still, are anxious about test-taking, and find everyday homework a real challenge. The Five Star Program® helps these students as long as they have a determination to do better. Those who are not motivated will need coaching and encouragement to start and, after a few days of doing the program reg-

---

1. To learn more about Janusz Korczak and Rudolf Steiner see pages 59-61.

2. See Bibliography, page 59, Korczak (1967), Educational Factors.

ularly, they will feel the difference and will be able to motivate themselves. **The key to this program is doing it, learning to be in the moment, observing how one feels and having fun.** When working with students please remember, any time the going gets tough, think—what can I do to make it easier and more fun?

The purpose of the Five Star Program® is to offer a **simple, five-step process** to help anyone (young or old) **improve academic performance, manage stress, foster a positive attitude towards learning and life in general.** Although this book is written for you, the teacher, to be able to bring the Five Star Program® to students, I highly recommend that you try it first on yourself. When you do the program yourself, you will see that it is **easy and fun.** With your newly gained confidence, you will be able to effectively bring it to your students. This program **helps your students assess themselves in a particular moment and take personal responsibility for their behavior and learning.** It has a positive effect on their self-esteem and helps them move towards becoming the person they choose to become.

This book introduces a simple process that improves performance for any student—those for whom learning is easy and those who have academic or behavioral challenges. It also **helps teachers to inspire their students to do better.** Students, younger than twelve, will need teachers or parents to help them learn it initially. If you are working with teenagers, you can suggest to them a teenage version of this book for their home use (The Five Star Program®: A Guide for Teenagers) to be published soon.

This is a DO BOOK. So you will need to get up, do what I suggest and test what I am proposing. Do it for at least three days in a row to gain confidence that the program works for you, before you bring it to your students.

May you enjoy the Five Star Program® and see its short and long-term benefits. If you find it helpful, share it with your colleagues, parents and friends. [3]

I wish for you a positive outcome as you explore this fun new way to approach your teaching, while at the same time helping young people become responsible for their own learning process.

---

3. For more suggestions on how to share the program, see page 57.

What is The Five Star Program®?

The Five Star Program® is a five-step process to help improve academic performance, manage stress, and foster a positive attitude towards learning.

It takes just a **few minutes** to do **twice a day,** and consists of the following simple steps (or "stars" since we are reaching for our highest potential):

1. **Vision:** Set a positive intention for the task you choose to do next.

2. **Movement:** Do four minutes of Brain Gym® [4] movements.

3. **Attention:** Give full attention to your task for the next 20 minutes.

4. **Take a Break:** Relax and integrate input from your senses in a specially designed area.

5. **Aerobic Exercise:** Vigorously walk or run (preferably outside) for 20 minutes per day.

> **✱Key Point:**
> Movement is needed for the brain to work effectively, efficiently, and with ease.

The following are good times to use the Five Star Program®:

- First thing in the morning, before starting school work.
- Before a class or test.
- Before homework, test preparation or test review.
- When students are in a bad mood, overwhelmed by their emotions, or losing their focus.

---

4. **Brain Gym®** (a registered trademark of the Educational Kinesiology Foundation) is a movement-based program that offers specific tools to enhance whole brain learning.

How to Use This Book

This book, Level 1, is simple. It explains five steps to be used in your classroom that take four to five minutes in total. To find out if the program could work in your classroom and for you (yes, the Five Star Program® is great for adults as well), first you need time to do the following:

1. Read Level 1 ➤ Part One once.

2. Read Level 1 ➤ Part One a second time. This time do all the five steps. Your intention for this activity could be:

    I am learning the Five Star Program® today with ease and I am having fun.

3. Repeat the Five Star Program® twice a day for at least three days. Your intention could be:

    I am getting more and more comfortable and confident with the Five Star Program®.

You can also try to use it before some specific activity:

    I am grading all the tests today in less than one hour and I have enough time for a nice walk with my family.

4. Introduce the Five Star Program® to your class.

5. When you and your class feel comfortable with Level 1 ➤ Part One, read Level 1 ➤ Part Two.

6. Incorporate each new instruction into your own daily routine and when you feel comfortable, introduce each new instruction to your students for at least five days.

7. In your spare time read Level 1 ➤ Part Three.

8. Most importantly—have fun!

Steps

Level 1 • Part One:
The Five Star Program®: Step by Step

In this section **you will learn how to do the set-up and use the Five Stars before and during tasks such as studying, doing homework, or reviewing for a test.** The material in this section (Part One) is stated in the simplest form possible so that you can follow it easily and do it right now. You may want to keep a daily journal with observations about your own experience with the Five Star Program®. Once you are comfortable with Part One and have introduced it to your class, you will find additional information for each Star in Part Two and you can incorporate this information when you are ready to go deeper into the program.

The Five Star Program®

☆1 **Vision:** Set intention(s).

☆2 **Movement:** Do Brain Gym® PACE.

☆3 **Attention:** Teach for 20 minutes.

☆4 **Take a Break** with the whole class or individual students.

Go back to ☆3.

☆5 **Aerobic Exercise**

Celebrate when done!

Set-Up: Getting Ready for the Activity
Setting Up the Room

Before we delve into the Five Star Program® itself, we set up the space where studying and breaks take place.

Since you want your students to study more effectively and with ease, **you can set up the space yourself or you can choose to do it with them.**

▶Air Out the Room.

If possible, air out the room for a few minutes before the class begins. You and your students will notice that the room "feels" cleaner and fresher. You may also check with students if they are too hot or too cold and let them adjust their clothing accordingly. When they are not comfortable, their performance will be affected even though they may not be aware of their discomfort.

▶Prepare Water.

Ask your students to bring their own water bottles or prepare a tray with paper cups filled with water for each student. Filtered water is preferred. Most students are dehydrated and yet will not drink water that tastes bad. If they ask for more than a cup of water, provide as much as they need. Their hydrated brains will work much better during the class. You will find additional information about water in Part Two, page 43.

▶Prepare the Take a Break (TAB) Area.

This is an area where your students take sensory breaks. The most appropriate spot is **away from the study area: a small table or a shelf is ideal.** Here are some suggestions for the TAB area. Put a nice piece of cloth on your table or shelf and place the following items on it:

◆ A little battery operated candle.

◆ An hourglass to keep time. You will decide how much time students are allowed for a break. One to three minutes is recommended.

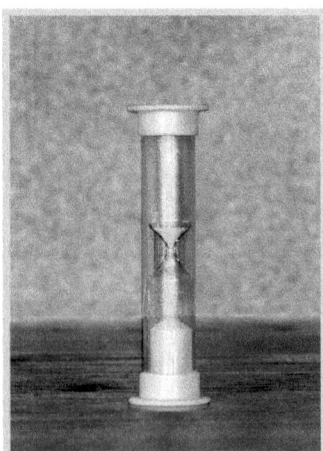

◆ A poster with the four Brain Gym® movements* or a copy of page 16.

The Brain Gym® PACE

1–Water

2–Brain Buttons

3–Cross Crawl

4–Hook-ups

Brain Gym™ is a registered trademark of the Educational Kinesiology Foundation.
This poster is from Mariola Strahlberg's book The Five Star Program. www.shiningmtnforkids.com. Poster format © Mariola Strahlberg 2015.

◆ Positive and encouraging words or sentences (you can find them in Part Two, page 38-39 or you can make them with your students).

◆ Photographs of nature related to different seasons.

◆ Red, green and blue colored paper. If you can take the time, it is wonderful for your students to make their own pictures by painting with red watercolor on the first day, blue on the second day, and green on the third day. The experience with each color is different and worth noticing. If you don't have the time, buy 8.5 by 11 inch colored paper. You can find additional

* To order, see Resources, #1, p. 61.

information about each color and its meaning in Part Two, page 36.

◆ Something from nature: a live plant, a bark of a tree, a feather, a rock, beach shells, or a crystal.

◆ To help your students "tune-up their brains," have them hold something soft in one hand and something hard or rough in the other. You can also use something heavy and something light, something big and something small.

◆ A stress ball.

◆ A kaleidoscope.

◆ A yoga ball instead of a chair.

◆ A yoga mat for movements to be done in a horizontal position or for taking a rest.

It may take you few days to collect these items. Students love to participate in creating the TAB area and have many ideas. They also like to change the space seasonally and bring their own "treasures" from home to share with their classmates.

Now that the TAB area is created, you are ready to experience the Five Star Program®.

Examples of the Take a Break Area

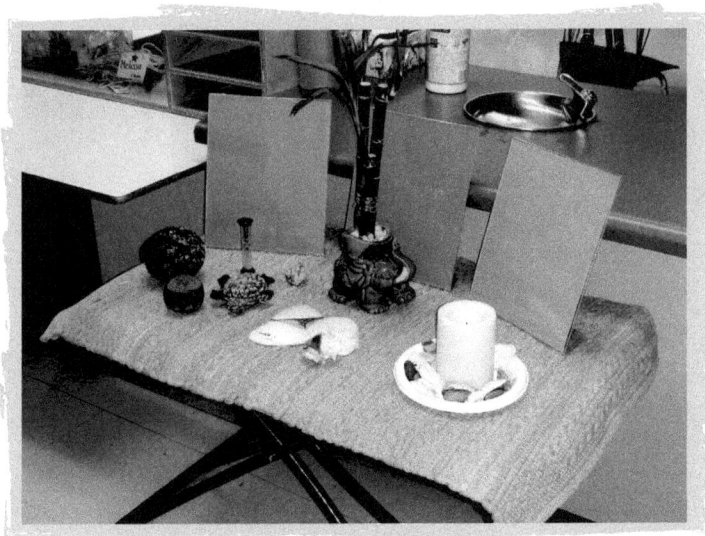

In a Kindergarten Class at Viola Elementary School, Suffern, NY

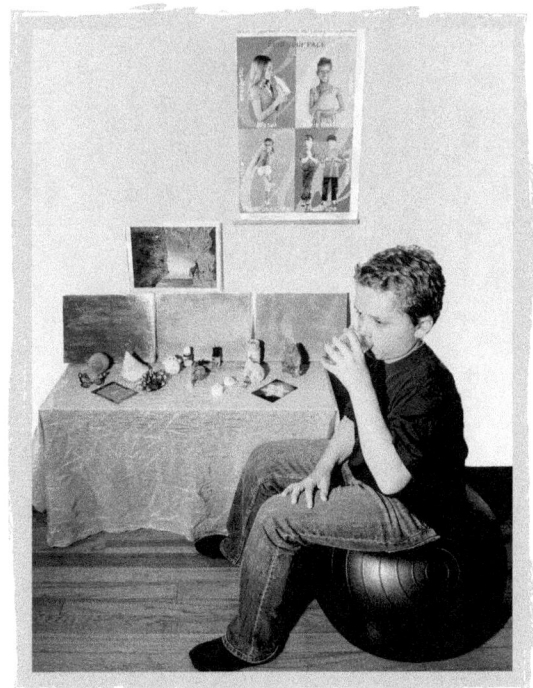

At the Shining Mountain Children's Center, Chestnut Ridge, NY

☆ Vision
Set an Intention for Your Activity

Intentions are written in the present tense as if they are happening now; they are positive and they start with "I." You cannot write an intention for anybody else but yourself. Here is an example of an **intention for a test preparation** that your students can set for themselves:

I stay focused and calm today while studying for my test, and I memorize the material with ease.

You can also set a separate **intention for yourself:**

I review the material with ease today. The class understands it well, and has fun.

Both intentions are written on the blackboard for everyone to see. In the future, when students are familiar with the Five Star Program®, they can **choose a leader each day** and then the leader decides with the class on the intentions and writes them down.

You may also choose to help your students to set **an intention for their review at home**. For example:

I stay focused and calm today while reviewing the test material and it takes me less than (specify time) hours to do it.

If there is time, your students may want to write their own intentions.

Some may like to write more than one intention and they are welcome to do that. Please make sure that their intentions are realistic. If they are not, have a discussion with them and help them modify their intention so that they are realistic and they can reach their goal and feel successful.

In the morning before the test, let your students set the intention for the test. Explain to your students that the fun part of setting intentions is to notice how often intentions come true, and therefore they can dream big. However, if they spent little time preparing, they cannot expect miracles! Teach your students to be honest and realistic with themselves while nurturing their self-esteem. Many students have an amazing ability to have their intentions come true even though they have not studied enough in your eyes. Therefore, make sure that you do not project your own expectations on them.

As an experienced teacher you know that many students get anxious before a test. Here are some examples of **intentions set before the test:**

> *I am calm, focused, and I do the test with ease in the allotted time,*
>
> or
>
> *I am calm, focused and I breathe deeply.*
>
> or
>
> *I have enough time and I get at least a B on my test.*

In the next section you will read about Brain Gym® activities and you will learn that doing Brain Gym® PACE is helpful before any activity including test taking. If there is not enough time before the test, at least set the intention, drink water and do Brain Gym® Hook-ups (more on that in the next section).

Intentions are also helpful when they are kept for a period of 21 days. There is a saying that it takes 21 days to break a habit. Let's assume your students have a big test three weeks from now. Your students can set an intention today, do the Five Star Program® for 21 days before daily review, see what their results are and notice how the process worked for them.

*Key Point:
Intentions are written in the present tense as if they are happening now; they're positive and they start with "I."

Here are three sample **intentions for test preparation** when the test will take place in the future:

I review test materials every day, for the next 21 days, from 7-8 pm.

I do the Five Star Program® and review 15 pages every day.

I stay calm, focused, and feel that I am getting better every day!

For more examples of intention setting, see Additional Information on Vision on page 41.

Congratulations—you have mastered the art of intention writing and you are ready to go to Star # ⭐2️⃣.

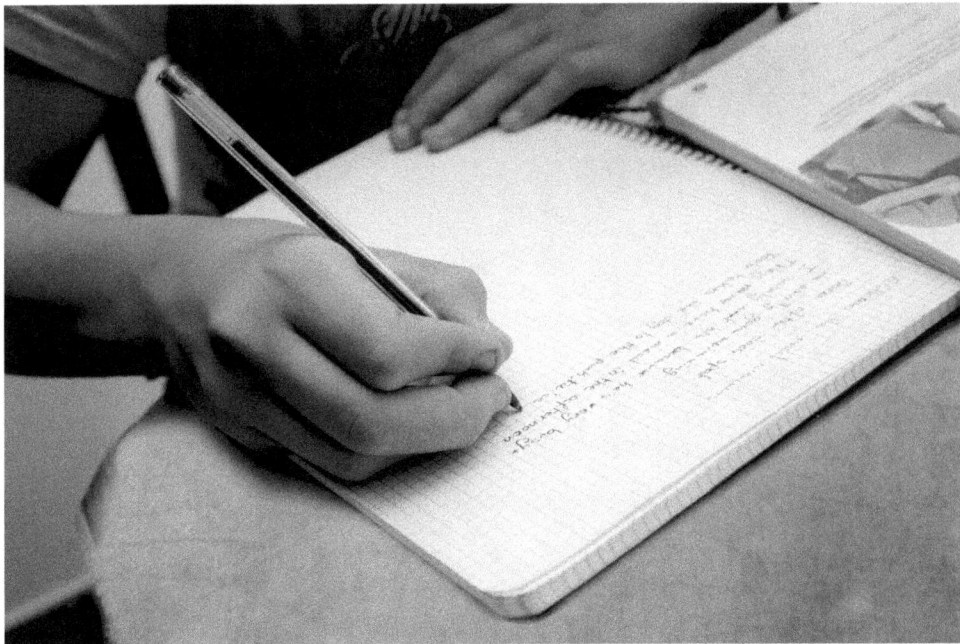

Setting Intentions

The Brain Gym® PACE

1–Water

2–Brain Buttons

3–Cross Crawl

4–Hook-ups

☆2 Movement
Brain Gym® PACE

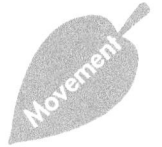

PACE is a movement sequence that prepares our body and brain for the activity that we are choosing to do. It does not matter if it is learning math, reading, writing, participating in sports or playing a musical instrument. We want to be ready for whatever we are going to do.

Let's look at the brain for a moment. Although some say that our brains are not just in our heads, today we will assume that they are. In simple terms, **the brain has two hemispheres,** right and left, each dedicated to specific tasks. In general terms, **the right hemisphere** gives us the possibility of seeing the big picture (i.e., the forest), versus **the left hemisphere,** which gives us the possibility of seeing the details (i.e., individual trees in the forest). When we use only one side of the brain, we get stuck either in the big picture or details. Using only one side of the brain gets us in trouble: we overreact, freeze or withdraw. Why do we use only one side of the brain? Some of the reasons may be due to being too tired, stressed out, dehydrated, or eating too much sugar. It is critical that both sides of the brain work together in order to have balanced mental and emotional

> **✦Key Point:**
> Just a few minutes of simple Brain Gym® movements increases focus and enhances performance.

reactions. With that in mind, let's prime the brain for the activity we are going to do next. You can look at PACE as a brain tune-up or warm-up.

Ask your students this question:

Are you ready (or are you "in PACE")

for the activity you are going to start?

For example,

Are you ready to start the review for

the test?

    or

Are you ready to listen to my lecture?

Are you in PACE?

Positive, **A**ctive, **C**lear and **E**nergetic?

There are four parts to PACE, and these four activities take about four minutes to do:

To be **Positive** we do an activity called Hook-ups,

To be **Active** we do Cross Crawl,

To be **Clear** we do Brain Buttons,

    and

To be **Energetic** we drink Water.

Let's start PACE now. We'll start at the bottom of the list and work our way up.

▶ Are you Energetic (Water)?

Ask your students to check in with themselves: Are you thirsty right now? Is your mouth dry? Is your body feeling restless or stiff?

We all need water to make electrical and chemical connections in the brain. Our muscles need water to feel flexible. Ask your students right now to drink at least ½ cup of water (four ounces), preferably filtered. Ask them also to notice their bodies' responses. With time they may find that the more they concentrate, the thirstier they get.

Water energizes our body and brain.

▶ Is your brain Clear (Brain Buttons)?

Ask your students if they feel alert and if their thinking is clear. Now ask them to stand up and place a thumb and forefinger of one hand **under** their collarbones. They will find small indentations ("Brain Buttons") right and left of their sternum. Let the other hand cover the belly button. Now let them **gently massage** the points under their collarbones for at least 30 seconds, while their other hand rests on the belly button. Make sure that everybody is breathing. Switch hands and repeat for 30 seconds.

Brain Buttons clear our brains and make us more alert.

▶ Are you **Active (Cross Crawl)?**

The Cross Crawl helps us cross the midline of our bodies. This is especially critical when we write, read or draw, since we have to cross the midline of our bodies with our eyes or hands. This activity takes one minute.

Ask your students to become aware if they are eager to learn, or if they are tired. Then instruct them in the following way:

While standing, place both hands on the

you hear everybody's feet hit the floor. Once everybody is able to start and stop at the same time, they can count out loud by 2s, 3s, 9s, up and down, repeat their multiplication tables, or practice their spelling words. The above variations of the Cross Crawl are done 60 times and take one minute.

Cross Crawl simultaneously activates both sides of the body and both brain hemispheres.

Cross Crawl Sequence

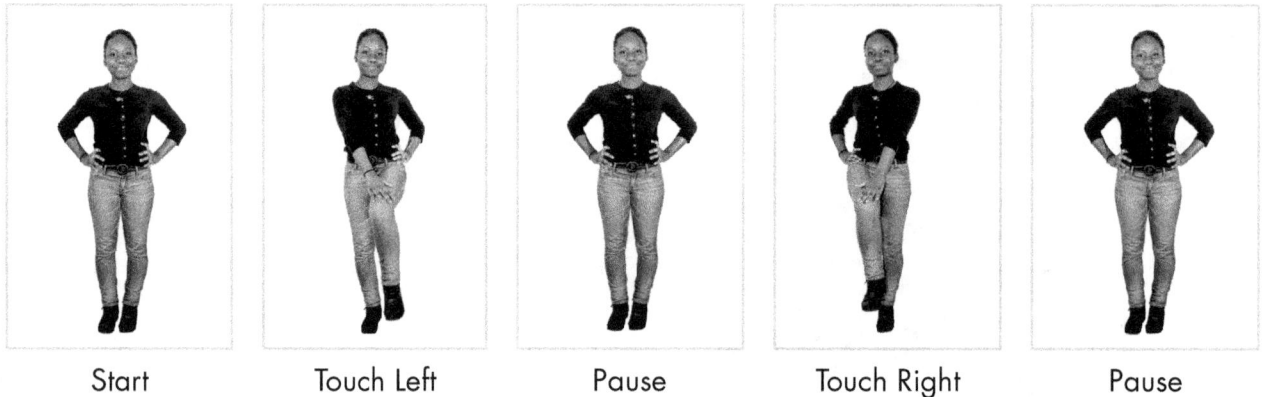

| Start | Touch Left | Pause | Touch Right | Pause |

waist. Raise the left leg and **touch the left knee with the right palm**. Return your legs and arms to the starting position, feet on the floor with both hands on your waist. Pause. Breathe... Repeat on the other side.

This time, raise the right leg and **touch the right knee with the left palm.** Pause.

Do this activity, switching hands and legs 60 times.

When doing Cross Crawl, your students may say to themselves or out loud: Front (when touching their knees), Pause (when they are still) till everybody is in sync and

▶ Are you **Positive (Hook-ups)?**

Ask your students if they feel optimistic and relaxed. When we are positive and relaxed it will be easier for us to achieve the best results in whatever we set our minds to do.

The Hook-ups activity can be done standing, sitting or lying down. Instruct students to **cross** their **right leg over** their **left leg** (see pictures) and extend both arms in front of them with thumbs pointing down. Then, take the **right hand and cross it over the left hand,** interlace fingers, tuck palms under and rest them on their chest. If that is not comfortable, they can rest them on their laps.

Ask students where their tongues are in their mouths. Is the tongue touching behind top teeth, hanging some place in the middle of the mouth or lying flat on the bottom of their mouths? Ask them to gently rest their tongues behind their top teeth keeping their mouths closed. Ask them to start taking deep, slow breaths. If they feel comfortable, they can close their eyes and imagine doing something that they love to do: climbing a mountain, reading a book, swimming, or playing a favorite sport. Do this for 30 seconds. Look at their faces. Are they beginning to relax?

Repeat this activity on the other side. Instruct students to **cross** their **left leg over** their **right** and extend both arms in front of them with thumbs pointing down. Take **left hand, cross it over right hand** and interlace fingers. Tuck palms under and rest them on their chest. Ask them to gently rest their tongues behind their top teeth. Start taking deep, slow breaths. With eyes closed or open, ask your students to imagine themselves doing

the activity they will be doing in a moment. If they are **preparing for a test,** let them see themselves turning pages in their practice book and checking off the questions they know. Let them see themselves feeling

Hook-ups Sequence (Right Over Left)

| Extend | Interlace | Tuck Under |

Hook-ups Sequence (Left Over Right)

| Extend | Interlace | Tuck Under |

happy and satisfied with their progress. If they are doing Hook-ups just before the test, let them see themselves understanding the questions, feeling relaxed, having enough time to complete the test. Let them see themselves handing their test back to you and feeling good about the whole experience. Do this for 30 seconds.

Now slowly unhook legs and hands, and bring palms together with the fingertips almost touching. Do they feel any tingling or warmth between their fingertips? If they do, let them move their palms slightly away and notice if they can still feel something. Ask them to breathe deeply and move their palms back and forth for 20 seconds.

How do your students feel now? How do you feel? Are you both relaxed, alert, and ready for your next step?

Hook-ups helps us feel calmer, deepens our breathing, and relaxes tension in our muscles.

PACE takes a little over four minutes and at the end of it, many students feel relaxed, positive and ready for the work ahead.

Are You in PACE?

Hook-ups
Positive

Cross Crawl
Active

Brain Buttons
Clear

Water
Energetic

Now you are finished with Movement and you are ready for Star # **3**.

☆3 Attention
Give Full Attention to a Task in 20-Minute Intervals

When do you pay 100% attention? Does it happen often? I bet it does. You do it when you are with friends and you totally forget yourself while listening to them. Or when you are listening to music or watching a movie and you are "one" with it; you are totally in the present moment. That is the type of attention you want your students to have when they are learning!

Much research points to the fact that **after 20 minutes our bodies need to move** and we need some **water to oxygenate the brain.** Our eyes need to see far into the distance after staring at a page, or need to shift to a closer focus after staring at a teacher or a blackboard. That is why it is good to **take short breaks** to recharge every 20 minutes. You know your students well—some lose their focus after five or ten minutes, others stay with you for 20 minutes. Wouldn't you choose to have them with you for the entire length of the class? Explain to your students that you will be doing your teaching in 20 minute intervals. Now ask your students to read their intention and start your class.

After 20 minutes, it would be ideal for the whole class to have a break for one to three minutes. They could drink some water and do one movement of your choice or their choice.

If that is not possible, consider allowing individual students to ask for a break at the Take a Break area.

If you or your students do not need a break, ask them to at least drink some water and do the next 20 minutes of teaching.

You are now ready for Star # ☆4.

At the Shining Mountain Take a Break Area

24

☆4 Take a Break
At a Designated Space for Movement, Sensory Integration and Relaxation

Allow individual students to **take a break after 20 minutes of intense studying.**

Let them drink some water, get up from their desk and walk to the Take a Break area. Let them turn the candle on, set the hourglass and do something that they feel drawn to do. They can look through the kaleidoscope, do some Brain Gym® movements, read an intention, or stretch up and down. Let them know that this short break will help them be calmer and ready to pay attention again. Let them repeat their intention. Repeating their intention tells their brain what they choose to accomplish.

Your students can also spend the time just sitting quietly at the Take a Break area, with their eyes closed or open, taking slow, deep breaths. When the hourglass is done, they can drink some more water, shut off the candle, repeat their intention(s) and go back to their desks ready to pay attention to you for the next 20 minutes.

In many schools, to hold students' attention, teaching is broken down into smaller mini-lessons. You will notice that taking a short break will bring large rewards in terms of your students' ability to focus and recall information.

At the Shining Mountain Take a Break area (opposite page), clockwise from top:
Cross Crawl on yoga mat; Hook-ups on yoga mat; Drinking water; Listening to the ocean/shell;
Smelling essential oil; Breathing deeply; Squeezing stress ball.

⑤ Aerobic Exercise
Move your Body

Dr. Paul Dennison, creator of the Brain Gym® program, coined two very pertinent sayings:

"Movement is the door to learning."
and
"Move to Learn and Learn to Move"

You may ask, why is movement important? **Movement** brings **oxygen to the brain, moves the lymphatic system, clears your head** and helps you look at your life situation in a more positive light. Doing movements outdoors adds more oxygen to your lungs and increases the brain's effectiveness. When intentions are set by your students before they begin aerobic exercise, they help clear your students' heads from the usual clutter of negative thoughts such as: *I can't do it; I'm not good enough; Nobody loves me; What's the use?*

Recommend to your students to do at least **20 minutes of aerobic exercise per day.** These 20 minutes can be split into two 10-minute or even four 5-minute intervals.

When the weather is nice, encourage your students to go outside and fast-walk, run, jump, skip rope, or play basketball before and

after school. It is as simple as that: let them get their pulse up, get their blood moving, let their lungs get some fresh air. Ask them to notice the trees and flowers around them and the color of the sky. This is also a wonderful exercise to do together with your class, time permitting. Just ten minutes, twice a day, and in a few days you will notice a big difference in how much more positive everyone is and how much more energy they have to do the work in front of them.

When **the weather is not nice** enough to go outside, twice a day, for 10 minutes, they can dance, skip, or run around the room, jump up and down or run up and down the stairs. If possible, remind them to open the window to get some fresh air. All they need to do is to move vigorously until their pulse is up and they feel out of breath.

You are now finished with the basic Five Star Program®. Time to reflect and celebrate!

Reflect and Celebrate

In life, we tend to wait for the big moments to celebrate: a birthday, graduation, a big game win. However, life is changing every day and there is always something to celebrate.

After a test or a project, it is good to reflect on it, to pay attention to what worked and what did not. When the same or similar situation occurs again, adjustments can be made.

You may choose to teach your students to **appreciate small victories,** like being able to write their paper in less than two hours, or preparing for a test and feeling that they know the material well. When we celebrate a small victory, we set ourselves up for another small victory the next time we sit down to do the activity. By celebrating, your students also learn to let go of the learning process and appreciate what they have learned.

Richard Buckminster Fuller once said: *"There is nothing in a caterpillar that tells you it's going to be a butterfly."* It's the same with your students. Neither you nor I know who your students will become and what kind of knowledge they will need. Therefore, everything they are learning may have a real-life application someday.

Celebrate with your students their little victories. Please don't skip this step. Teach your students to tell themselves: *I did well, I am proud of me.* You may also suggest to their classmates to compliment each other when they do good work. It is always nice to hear that we did something well since

we most often hear what we did not do well. If your students did not do well this time, suggest to them to tell themselves: *I know I can do better next time. I will study more or start studying earlier.* This will set the stage for a positive experience next time they sit down to study or take a test.

*Key Point

Teach your students to appreciate small victories. When we celebrate a small victory, we set ourselves up for another small victory the next time.

Quick Reference
for the Five Star Program®
Part One

To help you prepare for your first classroom experience with your students, here is a quick reminder list:

▶**Set-up:**
- ◆ Decide if you are going to be airing the room.

- ◆ Decide if students will be bringing water or set-up a tray with paper cups and a gallon of filtered water.

- ◆ Consider buying the PACE poster for your classroom, or copy page 16.

- ◆ Prepare your Take a Break Area. See ideas for items on page 10.

The Five Star Program®
A Simple Tool with Quick Results
Increases focus, motivation, ease of learning

The Five Star Program®

⭐ **Vision:** Set intention(s).

⭐ **Movement:** Do Brain Gym® PACE.

⭐ **Attention:** Teach for 20 minutes.

⭐ **Take a Break** with the whole class or individual students.

Go back to ⭐.

⭐ **Aerobic Exercise**

Celebrate when done!

The Five Star Program®

Set an intention for a task.

Perform a few simple movements.

Concentrate on a task for 20 minutes.

Take a short break.

Repeat till done.

Do 20 minutes of aerobic exercise every day.

Celebrate when done!

THE FIVE STAR PROGRAM®

Level 1 ◆ Part Two
Extra Ideas to Help You Succeed

In this section you will find additional information you can incorporate for each Star when you are ready to go deeper into the program.

In the **Set-up section**, you will learn how to enhance your experience with sound, color and essential oils.

In the **Vision section**, you will find additional information on setting intentions.

In the **Movement section,** you will find some simple tips how to help some of your students who are not able to do the simple movements you introduced to them.

In the **Take a Break section** you will find additional information on how to make this area special for your students.

In the **Aerobic Exercise section** you will find additional information on how to enhance your students' exercise program.

Extras

33

Additional Information
for the Set-Up

▶ Consider Enhancing Your Learning Environment With Sound

Many students learn much better when they have soft music playing in the background, while they are reviewing the material, reading or writing. There are many choices for the background music. There is a CD with specific music selections for Brain Gym® PACE which, while listened to when studying, have a similar effect on the brain as actually doing PACE movements (see page 60—Sound: Masgutova). There are selections of Baroque Music that evoke a specific psycho-physical state of relaxed concentration (see page 60—Sound: Ostrander) and Mozart's music was found to do the same (see page 60—Sound: Campbell). You can also consider a vast selection of nature sounds or music for relaxation. Find out what your students prefer. When you decide to use the music, prepare your equipment and order PACE CD from Shining Mountain (see page

61, Resource #3) or check various music selections mentioned in the books in the Sound section on page 60.

▶ Consider Enhancing Your Learning Environment with Essential Oils

Essential oils have been used for centuries for physical, mental and emotional wellbeing. There is research available on students' ability to focus better when studying and taking tests while using essential oils. (See page 61, Resource # 11.)

You can use the essential oils in many different ways. You can choose to use them in

More Set-Up

the Take a Break area. You can fill two small glass jars with Epsom salts and drop 2 drops of Peppermint Essential Oil in one jar and 2 drops of Lavender Essential Oil in the other jar and leave them on the table. You can also use them on the desks by dropping one drop of oil on a cotton ball. Another way to use the essential oils in the classroom is to use an aromatherapy diffuser. A diffuser purifies the environment and creates a pleasant atmosphere. Only one oil can be used in a diffuser at a time.

There are many brands of essential oils on the market. I only use Young Living essential oils and therefore all the instructions are with these oils in mind. I know that these particular oils are safe to inhale or put directly on your skin. I am not familiar with other essential oil brands.

When essential oils are on your fingers, keep them away from your eyes. If the essential oil gets into your eyes, you will need olive oil or any other cooking oil to "wash it off." Don't use water—water and essential oil do not mix!

How do your students choose an essential oil? Ask your students:

What do you need for your work?

*Do you need to **calm down?***
Then use Lavender Essential Oil.

*Do you need to **wake up and be more focused?***
Then use Peppermint Essential Oil.

For more information about essential oils, see page 60. For information on how to order essential oils, see page 61, Resource #5.

▶ Consider A Color Project For Your Students

In the Five Star Program®, we use three colors: red, green and blue. It is a special experience to paint for few minutes with each color on three different days and learn what the colors tell us and what effect they have on our mood and state of being. Painting with watercolors is preferable.

We have an intuitive sense of what color to use, and when to use it. What we may *not* be aware of is the fact that we choose the color of our clothing based on the energy we need (unless you dress according to the latest fad.) Your students may look at the color of a painting, have a specific colored tablecloth on the work table, wear a piece of clothing in a particular color or study under a colored light.

Here is some additional information about each color.[5]

RED connects us to the earth's energy, to the ground we stand on. Red energy is not in balance when we are fearful, tired or anxious. When we look at the color red, or wear red clothing, we bring in the qualities of **courage, self-confidence, love and will power** that we may need.

Red is our **creative energy**—your students need it to start a new project.

Recommend use of the red color to your students when they are tired, cold, lack courage or feel sorry for themselves. Once they choose the red color, they may use this intention:

I have courage today to do everything I choose to do.

BLUE takes us away from the ground into the vast sky and ocean; it gives us the sense that we are connected to the whole universe. Blue energy is not in balance when we are stressed out, in pain, emotionally unstable or unable to sleep. When we look at the color blue, or wear blue clothing, we bring in a **quality of calmness** to soothe our eyes and mind. If your students are restless, suggest that they study at home under blue light, or use a blue tablecloth on their desks.

Recommend use of the blue color when your students experience shock, or when they feel restless or emotionally unstable. Once your students choose the blue color, they may use this intention:

I am calm and able to share what I learn.

GREEN stands between red and blue. It is **harmonizing and balancing.** Green energy is not in balance when we have little control over our thoughts and actions, when we are angry or jealous, or always feel that we do not have enough (friends, money, good grades). Green is nature. People who mainly stay indoors lack what nature offers to them.

Recommend use of the color green when your students choose to have more **clarity** or **self-control or** want to feel more **sympathetic.**

Once they choose the green color, they may use this intention:

I feel peace and harmony in my heart, mind and body.

---

5. Information about color comes from An Introduction to Colour Energy® by I. Naess

▶Consider Enhancing Your Take a Break Area

▶**Leave a journal** for students to write down their thoughts while spending time in the TAB area. They can create a new intention or reflect on how they feel and write it in the journal.

▶**Create little squares of colored paper with positive words** and leave them in the TAB area. With time, your students can create their own positive words and share them with others. Positive words can be of great help when our minds are going in circles, or when we are upset or nervous about something. Instead of going over the same thoughts again and again, we can choose a positive word and repeat it to ourselves slowly, while we sit and breathe deeply. Suggest to your students to try this for at least 30 seconds while in the TAB area. Taking 30 seconds to do the positive word practice will clear their minds from the usual clutter of spinning thoughts. Here are some examples of positive words for you to start with:

▶**Create little pieces of paper with intentions** and leave them in the TAB area. What we pay attention to grows. Therefore repeating something positive motivates us to do our best. Here are some examples:

I choose to feel …happy, strong, etc….

I do my best.

Although I did not finish my work, I allow myself to take a short break and return to my work recharged and refocused.

I choose to stay calm, no matter what others say or do.

I take a few deep breaths and my body relaxes.

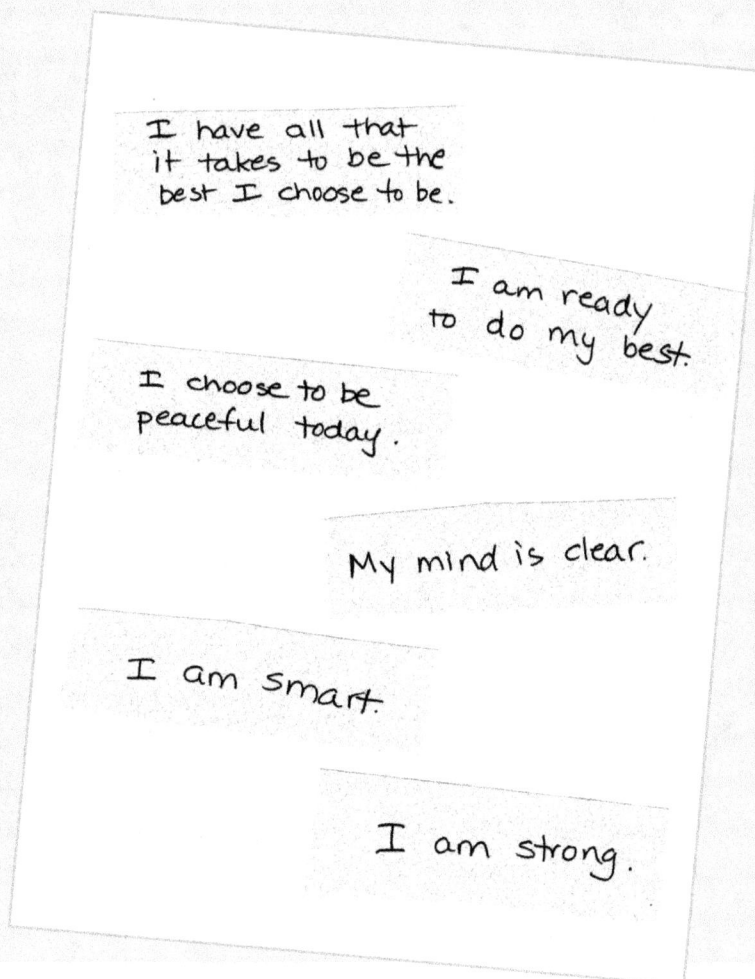

I have all that
it takes to be the
best I choose to be.

I am ready
to do my best.

I choose to be
peaceful today.

My mind is clear.

I am smart.

I am strong.

More
Take a Break

☆ Additional Information on Vision
Set an Intention for Your Activity

Working with intentions can be a very helpful practice to develop. To convince your students to do it, you can share with them a story of 14-year-old Mark, who did not think he was good in math.

Before each class or homework assignment, Mark repeated his favorite sayings: *I hate math,* or *I hate Mr. Jones, he is a terrible teacher, or math homework is a drag and it will take me forever!* As he learned the Five Star Program®, he began changing his intention to: *Math is fun today and I get it,* or *I do my math homework in one hour, I do it well and with ease.* You can imagine what happened next. In just a few months, from a C-minus student, he received B, B-plus, and A-minus, and moved to the advanced math group!

▶ Writing Intentions

The intentions listed here will give you an idea of how to help students to envision what they want and how to write their own intentions.

Before a class:
I pay attention to my teacher and learning today is fun.

Before a test while studying at home:
I study intensely without any interruptions for two hours and I feel good and well prepared for my test.

At the end of the day, to set a vision for the night:
I get a good night's sleep and wake up refreshed and ready to take the test.

Before a test in the classroom:
I stay calm, focused, do the test with ease, and finish on time.

Before a race:
I run effortlessly and reach the finish line in less than _____ minutes.

When things seem hard:
I choose to make it easy (easier).

When you tell yourself "I can't," "I don't care," or "I'm scared":
I can overcome the fear and move on.

More Vision

Making a "To Do List"

You may also guide your students to create a list of what they need to do today in order to prepare for tomorrow's test. Here is an example of a "To Do List:"

1. I go running for 10 minutes or do Brain Gym® PACE.

2. I see how long my test preparation takes:
   Activity start time: _____

3. I set my intention for test review.

4. I go over the review material for 20 minutes without interruptions.

5. I take short breaks every 20 minutes.

6. I stay focused, calm, and positive.

7. Activity end time: _____
   Total test review time: _____

8. I drink and eat just enough food so that my body is happy and able to feed my brain well. I drink only water or green tea, and eat plenty of vegetables, fruit and protein instead of sugary snacks, salty chips or chocolate.

9. I get 10.5 hours of sleep tonight and wake up rested, positive and ready for the test.

Now your students are ready to create their own "To Do Lists."

☆2 Additional Information on Movement
Brain Gym PACE®

In this section you will find information on how to make PACE easier for those students who are having a difficult time doing the movements.

You will also find some information that may be helpful to you for explaining to students why these movements improve brain functions.

▶ Water to Energize Your Brain and Your Body

Ask your students to check in with themselves: are they thirsty right now? Are their mouths dry? Are their bodies feeling stiff?

The amount of water in the human body averages from 50–75%, while the brain is 75–85% water. Any academic activity "exercises" our brain and our brain needs water to make all the necessary connections, otherwise it will shrink like a grape that is exposed to sun and become a raisin!

How much water is a good amount for us to drink daily? Some people recommend taking your weight in pounds and dividing it into half. That's the amount of water in ounces that is good for our bodies. If you divide this amount by eight ounces, you will know how many cups your students need to drink per day. It is important to **drink extra water before a test, when students are stressed out or when they are sweating.**

If a student does not like to drink water, suggest adding some lemon or grapefruit juice to it. Ask them to drink at least ½ cup (four ounces) of filtered water before they begin studying, and let them repeat drinking water every 20 minutes during their study time.

Do your students like the taste of their water? I had an interesting experience with a group of school children during their summer remedial program. The first time I asked them to drink water, nobody moved. The teacher pointed out to me that the school water does not taste very good. So the next

More Movement

time I came to the class, I brought a gallon of filtered water. And what do you think happened? I did not have enough water for the 24 children in the class! They were thirsty—very thirsty—and they loved the good-tasting water. Make sure that the water tastes good and your students will drink as much as they need without having to be asked to do it.

▶ Brain Buttons to Clear Our Brains and Make Us More Alert

Massaging the soft tissue under the clavicle to the right and left of the sternum sends messages to the right and left hemisphere of the brain, brings more oxygen to the brain and stimulates the carotid artery for increased supply of blood to the brain. This simple activity improves **eye teaming skills, relaxes neck and upper shoulder muscles, helps with number and letter reversals and enhances energy level.** Massage Brain Buttons gently, as these points will sometimes be tight or painful. If they are, it may be because your students are stressed, anxious, or they did not get enough sleep. Let them massage the points and notice if the tenderness is released. While massaging the Brain Buttons, let them count to 30 (*1 and 2 and 3 and …30 and*) and then switch hands and repeat counting backwards

this time.

Notice if your students are able to do the movements without squinting their eyes or moving their mouth. When they do not squint or move their mouths, they are ready for their eye tracking exercises. Buy blue and red ribbons, 3 yards long and 1.5 inches wide, and hang them some place below the ceiling in a horizontal direction on opposite sides of the room. While doing Brain Buttons, let your students turn to the wall with their chosen color and move their eye horizontally. Switch hands and repeat. This activity **helps with crossing the visual midline for reading.** You will notice that the students who need to wake up will turn to the red ribbon and the ones who are anxious or restless will turn to the blue ribbon.

▶ Cross Crawl to Feel Active and Ready for the Activity

Cross Crawl is a contralateral exercise that accesses both brain hemispheres simultaneously. This is a perfect warm-up activity for the brain because when we write, read, or draw we need to cross the body's midline. While doing this activity, your students can practice counting up and down, doing their multiplication tables or spelling words. They can do the following variations:

Front – Pause – Front – Pause (use palm)

Front – Pause – Front – Pause (use elbow)

Back – Pause – Back – Pause

Back – Front – Pause – Back – Front – Pause

Side – Pause – Side – Pause

Front – Side – Pause – Front – Side – Pause

Front – Back – Side – Pause – Front – Back – Side – Pause

To improve balance, students can also do Cross Crawl with closed eyes, or walk or skip while doing them.

Most of your students will have no problem doing this activity. However, you may find a few who will consistently touch their right hand to their right knee and are not able to move across the midline of their bodies. The older the students, the more embarrassed they will be. Here are some suggestions for these students. You may suggest to them to practice Cross Crawl at home by:

◆ Putting a sticker on their right palm and the same sticker on the left knee and matching the stickers. Then touching the sides without the stickers.

◆ Doing Cross Crawl lying down.

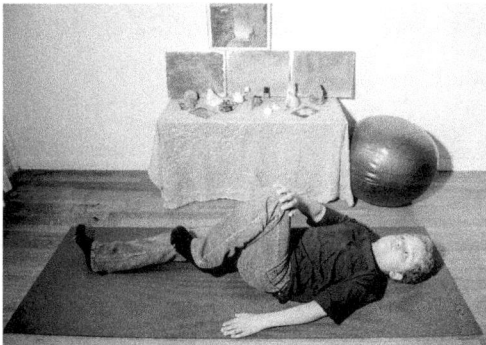

◆ Doing Cross Crawl in front of a mirror.

◆ While sitting at a table with both palms on the table, lift right palm and touch the left knee, return both palms to the table, repeat on the opposite side.

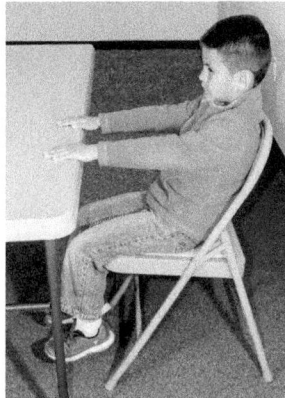

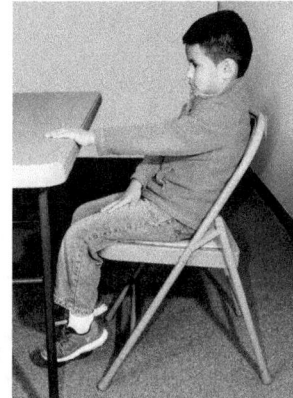

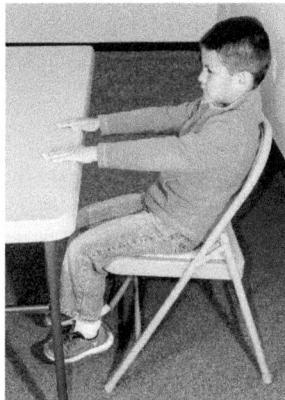

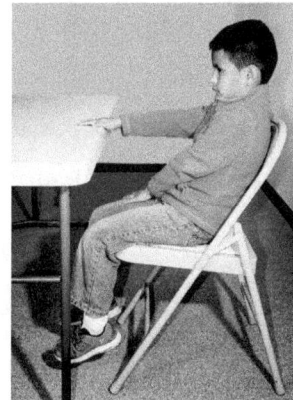

▶ Hook-ups to Be Positive and Relaxed

Hook-ups shift electrical energy from the hindbrain (flight and fight brain) to the neocortex (executive brain). The tongue pressing into the roof of the mouth stimulates the limbic system for emotional processing in concert with reasoning centers in the frontal lobes. Hook-ups can be done standing, sitting or lying down. They **improve balance and coordination, self-control and comfort in the environment, and deepen respiration.**

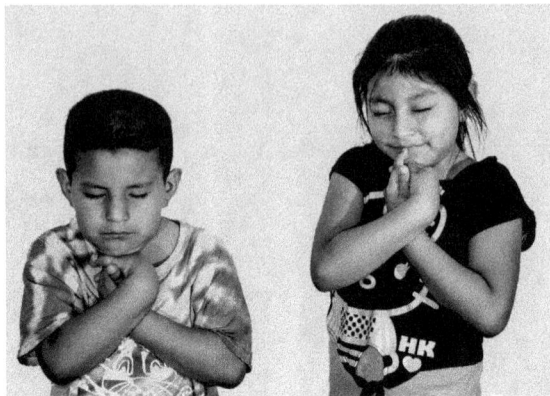

The figure 8 pattern of the arms and legs follows the energy flow of the body allowing for relaxation, grounding and increased attention.

When the students touch their fingertips in Part Two of Hook-ups, their two brain hemispheres get connected and balanced.

Before a test or when feeling anxious, you can suggest to your students to sit in Hook-ups with their hands interlaced and resting on their laps. After just a few moments they will feel more relaxed.

If you would like to learn more about Brain Gym®'s effect on young learners, special-ed learners, or adult learners, you can find some research on page 61, Resource #9.

Please note:

If you are teaching in a Waldorf or Montessori School or you know specific movements that have a positive effect on body and mind that increase focus, motivation and overall calmness, feel free to substitute them for Star #2: Movement in The Five Star Program® and see for yourself if they make a difference in your students' lives.

☆3 Additional Information on Attention
The Two Selves

People sometimes feel like there are two of them: one who makes decisions that help them in their lives, and the other one who makes decisions just for this moment in time.

The first part of them—the one that knows what is right for them—does not mind hard work. Every time this part is faced with material that seems boring, it sees it as a challenge and an adventure: *What if, in the material I am going to study, there is something that will give me an answer I have been struggling with, or show me a direction I may take in the future?*

The second part likes to have a lot of time to do nothing, or do things that are easy and fun, or eat foods that are very tasty but not healthy. Let us call the first part a "higher self," and the second part a "lower self." You can explain these two selves to your students and ask them to invite their higher self to join them today. With their higher self in charge, they will have **self-discipline** and

motivation for the next 20 minutes of studying. Ask them to read their intention again. If they are still balking at the idea, ask them to motivate themselves and notice that studying will take less time today, will be easier and more satisfying for them.

Now they are ready to proceed with their work

▶ Self-Assessment

After about 20 minutes, you can suggest to your students to ask themselves a few simple questions:

- ◆ Am I thirsty?
- ◆ Do I need to move a bit?
- ◆ Am I getting restless?
- ◆ Do my eyes need to look at something away from the printed page or the blackboard?
- ◆ Is my attention as strong as it was 20 minutes ago?

Self-assessment is an important skill to learn. Once your students know how to do it,

49

they will not need a teacher or a parent to tell them that they are not paying attention, moving too much, disturbing others, or day-dreaming. They will know themselves and they will be able to take care of their own needs. By taking a short break after 20 minutes and **performing a short self-assessment, they are taking responsibility for themselves.** There is no need for somebody to nag them or tell them what to do; they are making conscious decisions for themselves. Some students will need a break after 20 minutes, others may be fine for 30 minutes or longer. With your help, they are able to assess themselves and decide what they need to do to be more effective learners.

⭐ Additional Information on Take A Break

A nice addition to the Take a Break area is a journal. In it, before taking a break, your students can write their name, date and how they feel. They may answer the following questions:

How is my body feeling? (hot, sluggish, thirsty, hungry), other feelings:

How is my brain feeling? (foggy, clear, thoughts are running back and forth, focused), other feelings:

How much work did I do so far?
How did my studying go? Did I understand the material well?

If sitting in class today is difficult for them, taking a break, drinking some water, doing one or more movements is helpful before they resume their participation in the class.

I find that many students appreciate the Take a Break area. They like to decorate it themselves and change it from time to time.

Take a Break at home

Many students take the idea with them and create their own TAB areas at home.

51

Here are some comments about TAB from fourth and fifth grade students at the Viola Elementary School in Suffern, New York:

Dear Ms. Mariola,

Thank you for coming into our class. It helps me go into learning land. My favorite move that we do is hookups. Hookups help me to focus and concentrate, it also helps me feel relaxed after many tests. I like the new versions of cross crawls that you keep teaching us. Brain buttons help me wake up and calm down if I need to. My favorite thing you had us do was the massage train because it really hits the spot when I am stressed out on a test. This is a amazing process.

Your Student
Emma

Dear Ms. Mariola,

When I do Hookups I feel myself that I'm relaxing. Because it so quiet that I feel I'm sleeping!! When my class is at a spa!! When I do the massage train I feel I'm at a spa!! When I do the cross crawls I feel pumped to do them because when I'm tired it wakes me up. I hope you can teach us move.

From Edgar

Dear Mariola,

Thank you for makeing my class a part of the 5 ★★★★★ Star program. It Helps Me Relax. I Hope you come Back soon!! I Love cross Crawl. I know my 7 time tables 7,14,21,28,35,42, 49,56,63,70,77,84! I did it. TO Impore th TABA Jake a break area. I think we sould have music and paintings. I Love The take a break area! I use hookups at the cross country race and at my play this weekend!

P.S. I think We sould have guided Imgry

Love ♥ ♥ ♥
Julia

Dear Ms. Mariola, 3/25/15

Our time to relax and move around is awesome. Being able to let my body go loose after a test is like a dream. The whiskers, the brain buttons, the skips, the hookups and the massage train all fit this time perfectly. My favorite is the massage train because it relaxes me and allows me to have fun at the same time. They even allow me to ... Show my inner-peace ...
... Trey

Dear Ms. Mariola 3/25/15

This program has brought me to the stars. I have been very thankful we had the opportunity to do this program. When ever I am stressed I do a hook up. It is probably my favorite thing in the program but I do love the massage train. These two things help me find my inner peace. Cross crawls let me just loosen up so I can get the stress off my back from a desk. Brain buttons are really like buttons after work. I'm tired and then it makes my brain warm up for more work. Whiskers help me for my concentration to be precise and eager. This program Really is Five Stars.
From, Alica

"*Thank you for using your time to come to our class and helping us to be more relaxed during work. I really like the TAB area and I even made a break area at home.*"

"*Thank you very much for coming into our classroom, This made me more relaxed and less frustrated. Now I made the relaxation station (take a break area) at home in my room.*"

"*Thanks for coming in and teaching us the Five Star Program®. Trust me it has been really helping. I use it everywhere I go: home, school, doctors. I used to stress a lot but now since I have the Five Star it really helps me. I made my own relaxation area and I love it soooooooooo much.*"

THE FIVE STAR PROGRAM®

★ ★ ★
★   ★

⑤ Additional Information on Aerobic Exercise

With recent decreases in the amount of time students spend in recess and gym, there is an avalanche of articles about the **effect of physical activities on the brain, mood, weight and health.** In the Resource section you can find references to articles on that subject (see page 61, Resources #6 and #7).

Doing aerobic exercise with a specific intention clears your students' heads from the usual clutter of negative thoughts. Before doing the exercise, ask your students to answer two simple questions that will help them set intention(s) for the activity:

◆ How are you feeling right now? (Circle all that apply.) Positive, motivated, ready to study, energetic, tired, cranky, upset that I have to study, hungry, distracted, have a headache, thirsty, anything else:

◆ How would you like to feel? (Circle all that apply.) Positive, motivated, ready to study, energetic, anything else:

Now ask them to set the intention for aerobic exercise. For example:

I move my body and breathe deeply to learn with ease for my math test.

Write down your intention:

Remind them to repeat their intention as they do their aerobic exercise. They can repeat it all the time or only when they notice their minds going back to their negative thoughts. When they are back from their exercise, ask them to answer these two simple questions:

◆ How are you feeling right now? (Circle all that apply.) Positive, motivated, ready to study, energetic, tired, cranky,

More Exercise

upset that you have to study, hungry, distracted, have a headache, thirsty, anything else:

◆ Were you able to repeat your intention while doing the aerobic exercise?

If they were not able to quiet their minds, ask them what was going on in their heads. With practice, they will be able to let go of the mental clutter and give their brains a well deserved rest. Impossible, they say? Well, here are two other suggestions. **While running or walking,** they can pick one word that inspires them and repeat it to themselves while doing the activity. They can also pick a melody and put some positive words into it. Ask them to sing it to themselves as they run or walk.

For example, use the tune of "Frère Jacques—Brother John:"

I am healthy,
I am happy,
I am strong,
I am smart,
I can focus better,
Math is easy for me,
I do well,
I feel proud.

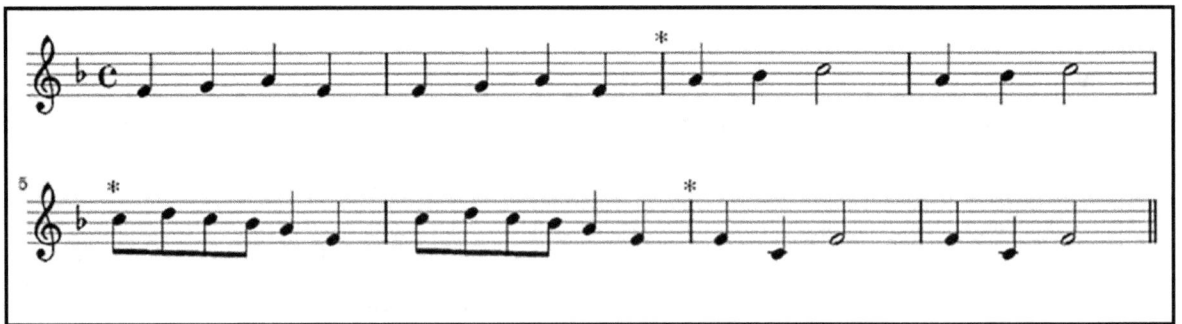

Melody – Frère Jacques

Quick Reference
for the Five Star Program®
Part Two

After you have practiced the Five Star Program® with your students for a few days, and you are ready to add extra ideas from Part Two, this quick reference can be used as a reminder checklist.

▶ **Set-up:**
- Air out your classroom.

- Order red and blue ribbons for Brain Buttons and hang them on the opposite sides of the classroom.

- Once you decide to use Brain Gym® music, prepare CD player and order CD. See page 61, Resource #3, for ordering information.

- Once you decide to use essential oils, see page 61, Resource #5, for order information.

- Talk to your art teacher and ask to do a color project with your students—see page 36 for details.

- Talk to your music teacher to help your students with a special class song for Cross Crawl.

- Consider asking students for suggestions for the classroom's Take a Break area.

- Suggest to your students that they set up a TAB area at home.

The Five Star Program®
A Simple Tool with Quick Results
Increases focus, motivation, ease of learning

The Five Star Program®

☆1 **Vision:** Set intention(s).

☆2 **Movement:** Do Brain Gym® PACE.

☆3 **Attention:** Teach for 20 minutes.

☆4 **Take a Break** with the whole class or individual students.

Go back to ☆3.

☆5 **Aerobic Exercise**

Celebrate when done!

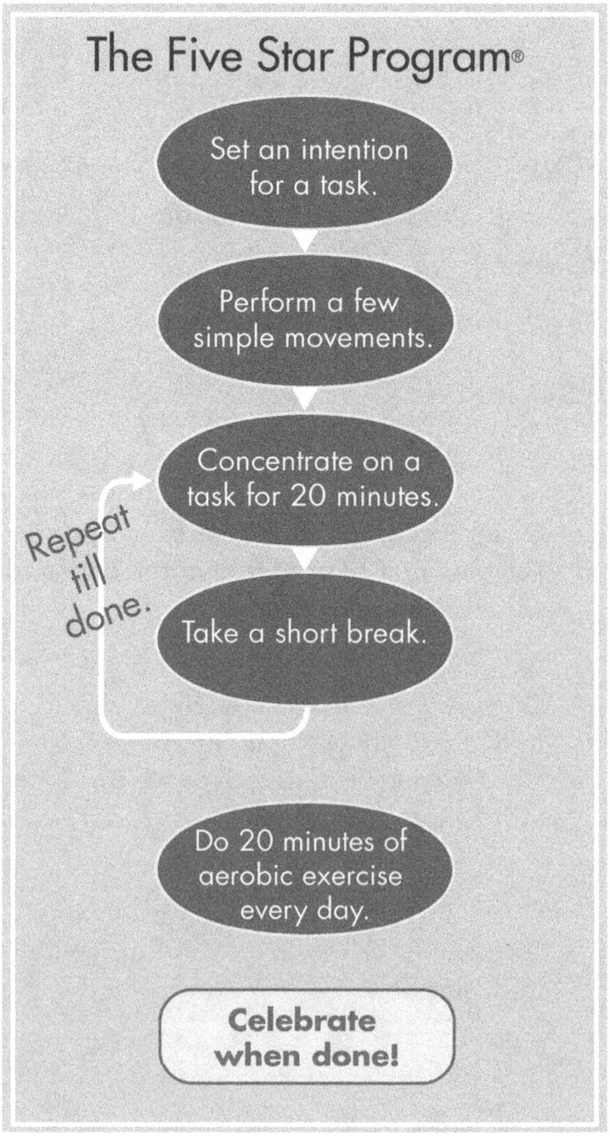

The Five Star Program®

Set an intention for a task.

Perform a few simple movements.

Concentrate on a task for 20 minutes.

Take a short break.

Repeat till done.

Do 20 minutes of aerobic exercise every day.

Celebrate when done!

Level 1 ◆ Part Three
Final Thoughts

Congratulations! You have read Level 1, Parts One and Two, of this book and experienced the Five Star Program®.

Over the years, I have observed amazing changes in students' performance and behavior in only a matter of 21 days when these simple steps are practiced twice a day for just a few minutes at a time.[6] **The Five Star Program® can benefit people of all ages, from pre-kindergarten to adult.** After using it for some time, many **college students** report reduced anxiety and better results on their tests, parents of **kindergarten children** notice better sleep and behavior in their five year-olds, and **seniors** feel more alert and positive. **The Five Star Program® can be used in a classroom, an after school program, and at home or work.** You can use it with the whole class, or if you are a special education teacher or a social worker, you can use it with individual students.

▶Why the Five Star Program®?

The moment I read Janusz Korczak's *How to Love a Child* (1914) and *The Child's Right to Respect* with its *Declaration of Children's Rights* (1929), I knew I needed to develop the program. Here are some of the rights Korczak felt children should have:

The child has the right to respect,
The child has the right to be herself or
  himself,
The child has the right to live in the
  present,
The child has the right to make mistakes,
The child has the right to be taken seriously.

The Five Star Program® allows students to take personal responsibility for their learning process and encourages their teachers to guide them. Once your students feel comfortable with the Five Star Program®, here is my wish for them. After they see and feel the results, large or small,

Final Thoughts

---

6. See reference on page 61, Resource #8, to my article about the East Ramapo Summer Program experience.

wouldn't it be nice to share this new knowledge with others? There is a saying, *It doesn't matter what you have; what matters is how much you give.* Encourage your students to share the Five Star Program® with their families and friends, and look for ways to teach it to another class in their school.

Your students can volunteer in an after-school program or a library. There are many children who do not see their parents until late at night. They spend many hours after school in various centers; these centers are a great place for your students to volunteer. They could bring the Five Star Program® to these children. They could go running with these children, help them with their homework, be a role model. Once they do something like that, please ask them to write to us at www.shiningmtnforkids.com. Look for the tab "Kids Helping Kids" and let them register there. They will be able to share their experiences with others who like to help. When you find young people who out of their own initiative do something special for others, please let us know about them. Once a year, we give out the Janusz Korczak Spirit Award to one special young person to perpetuate the legacy of Korczak and his children (to read about Korczak and his children, read Betty Lifton's book, *The King of Children*).

If you would like to learn more about Korczak's educational model of a democratic republic and how you can implement it in your classroom, you can contact Mariola at the Janusz Korczak Association of the USA. Established in New York City in 2013, the US Association has been a member of the International Korczak Association with members from 25 countries. The Korczak educational model can be found in many schools in Poland, Russia, France, Israel, Finland, Japan and even Ivory Coast. The US Association is working to bring Korczak's ideas to the United States via lectures, exhibits and the Five Star Program®. (See page 61, Resource #10, for additional information).

Young people can make a difference in education. There is power in numbers. Guide your students to be courageous, to share what they know and what has helped them. Teach them to believe in themselves and to enjoy their life experiences.

Bibliography

General

Goddard, S. (2002). *Reflexes, Learing and Behavior—A Window into the Child's Mind*, Fern Ridge Press.

Hartmann, T. (2004). *The Edison Gene: ADHD & The Gift of the Hunter Child*, Inner Tradition.

Kuhlewind, G. (2004). *Star Children—Children Who Set Us Special Tasks and Challenges*, Temple Lodge Publishing.

Louv, R. (2005). *Last Child in the Woods: Saving Our Children From Nature-Deficit Disorder*, Algonquin Books.

Korczak

Bogacki, T. (2009). *The Champion of children: The story of Janusz Korczak. New York: Farrar*, Straus & Giroux.

Efron, S. (2005). *Janusz Korczak: Legacy of a Practitioner-Researcher. Journal of Teacher Education, 56* (2), 145-155. DOI:10.1177/0022487104274415.

Engel, L.H. (2008). *Experiments in Democratic Education: Dewey's Lab School and Korczak's Children's Republic. Social Studies, 99, (3)*, May/June, 117-121.

Korczak, J. (1967). *Educational factors (J. Bachrach, Trans. In M. Wolins (Ed.). Selected works of Janusz Korczak (pp 1-80)*. Washington, DC: National Science Foundation. (Original work published 1919).

Korczak, J. (1967). *How to love a child (J. Bachrach, Trans.). in M. Wolins (Ed.), Selected works of Janusz Korczak (pp 81-462)*. Washington, DC: National Science Foundation. (Original work published 1914).

Korczak, J. (1992). *When I Am Little Again;* and, *The Child's Right to Respect* (E.P. Kulawiec, Trans.) Lanham: University Press, 1992. (Original work published 1925, 1929).

Lifton, B.J. (1988). *The King of Children: A Biography of Janusz Korczak,* New York: Farrar, Straus and Giroux.

Steiner

Petrash, J. (2002). *Understanding Waldorf Education – Teaching from the Inside Out*, Gryphon House.

Steiner, R. (1995). *The Kingdom of Childhood —Introductory Talks on Waldorf Education*, Anthroposophical Press. (Original work published in 1924).

Montessori

Seldin, T. (2006). *How to Raise An Amazing Child the Montessori Way*, DK Publishing.

Brain Gym®

Brown, K. (2012). *Educate Your Brain*, Balance Point Publishing.

Cohen, I & and Goldsmith, M. (2002). *Hands On: How to Use Brain Gym® in the Classroom*, Educational Kinesiology Foundation.

Dennison, P & Dennison, G. (1989, 1994, 2010). *Brain Gym® Teacher's Edition,* Hearts at Play, Inc.

Dennison, P & Dennison, G. (1986). *Brain Gym®—Simple Activities for Whole-Brain Learning,* Edu-Kinesthetics, Inc.

Hannaford, C. (2005). *Smart Moves: Why Learning Is Not All In Your Head,* Great River Books.

Color

Dinshah, D. (2000). *Let There Be Light,* Dinshah Health Society.

Mandel, P. (1986). *Practical Compendium of Colorpuncture,* Freiburger Graphische Betriebe.

Naess, I. (1996). *Colour Energy,* Colour Energy Corporation.

Naess, I. (2004). *An Introduction to Colour Energy®,* Colour Energy Corporation.

Essential Oils

Essential Oils Desk Reference, 6th edition. (2014). Life Science Publishing.

Sound

Campbell, D. (1997). *The Mozart Effect,* Avon Books.

Carey, D and Muynck, M. (2002). *There is no place like Ohm,* Devachan Press.

Masgutova, S. (2003, 2005). *Music For Everyone® PACE CD or Get Ready to Learn CD,* www.masgutovamethod.com

Ostrander, S & Schroeder, L. (1979). *Super Learning,* Dell Publishing Co.

Resources

1. To order Brain Gym books and products (PACE posters and bookmarks), visit www.braingym.com.

2. To learn about Brain Gym® courses and research, visit www.braingym.org.

3. To order CD with music for Brain Gym® PACE, please call Shining Mountain at 845-425-7243 or email us at shiningmtnny@aol.com.

4. To order books about essential oils, visit www.lifesciencepublishers.com.

5. To order essential oils from Young Living, visit www.youngliving.com and use Mariola's number to order (172520) or call Shining Mountain at 845-425-7243.

6. To learn more about Fitness Breaks in School, visit www.actionforhealthykids.org for many references for classroom activity breaks, content learning with movement, yoga programs, etc.

7. For reference to articles and studies published by various national organizations on the effect of movement on children's health and school performance, contact Rockland County School Health and Wellness Coalition at www.rocklandsteps.org.

8. To learn more about effect of Brain Gym® on the East Ramapo students in their summer remedial program, see my article, *Finding Our PACE In Summer School* in Brain Gym Journal, December 2009, Volume XXIII, No. 3, page 11.

9. To learn more about the effects of Brain Gym® on different learners, see Kathy Brown's book, *Educate Your Brain,* pgs 36-38.

10. To learn more about Janusz Korczak Association of the US, please visit www.facebook.com/korczakUSA or call Mariola at 845-425-7243.

11. To learn more about the effects of essential oils on attention, see the article at http://shiningmtnforkids.com/adhd-study.pdf

Resources

Afterword

One of the most rewarding moments in author's life is when a reader actually reads the afterword. To me it means that the whole book was read and there is interest to hear more. After 16 years of working with children, plus another 25 years or raising my daughter and working in the corporate computer field, of course I have much more to say.

Now that you have learned the basic Five Star Program®, how can you use it? You can use it in the classroom and also for yourself. If you have parents who would like to help their children, you could suggest to them to read the book and use it with one child instead of the whole classroom. I will consider rewriting this book and making it a parents' guide when many parents ask for it.

What about your friends and spouses? They certainly can use it when they are stressed out about giving a talk, making a phone call, writing a paper, analyzing data. Everybody knows that being relaxed benefits any life situation, and writing an intention makes it happen. (Check out books by Napoleon Hill, Claude Bristol, and James Allen if you need convincing).

What about teenagers? Well, I am working on the e-book for teenagers. To condense 70 pages into few pages is not easy but I am determined to do it. I am also planning to publish Level II of this book with a special section dedicated to test-taking and more in depth ideas for the classroom to help young people specifically with reading, handwriting (yes, the forgotten skill of handwriting so important for our brains), memorizing, and public speaking. There will also be a section for pre-K and kindergarten children.

Currently I offer retreats, lectures and workshops and will be happy to come to your place of work to talk about the Five Star Program®. If your organization is interested in doing a formal study on the Five Star Program®, I would be interested in exploring it further with you. If you don't have time for all that, we can arrange a webinar in which you can ask your questions and explore the Five Star Program® in more depth. Here are the ways you can reach me:

- ◆ Call me at 845-425-7243,
- ◆ Email me at shiningmtnny@aol.com or shiningmtnma@aol.com.

About the Author

Over the years, Mariola Strahlberg has met many children and their parents in her private practice and at schools, afterschool programs and camps. When she is with a child, she takes her time observing and processing until she understands not only with her head but with her heart. At Shining Mountain, each child is approached individually: strengths are encouraged and developed while deficits and difficulties are noted. Mariola uses a comprehensive, integrated approach that allows each child to see visible progress in a matter of weeks while parents benefit from learning what makes their children succeed in various areas of their lives.

Mariola was lead to work with children during her daughter's school years when she witnessed the struggles many children had at school. She dreamed of starting a center where helping children discover their unique capabilities would be implemented through use of natural modalities. After pursuing a successful career of 25 years in the corporate computer field at Bell Laboratories and Telecom Italia, she earned her Master's of Science in Acupuncture with honors from Tri State College of Acupuncture in June, 1999. She has been in private family practice (Shining Mountain Acupuncture, LLC) in Rockland County, NY since then. She has extensive training in the application of color, movement, therapeutic grade essential oils and tuning forks in Oriental Medicine.

In 2004, Mariola founded Shining Mountain Children's Center. In 2007, she opened Shining Mountain Center for Peaceful Childhood, Inc., a not-for-profit company that brings the Five Star Program® to schools and provides scholarships to children who would otherwise not be able to attend the program.

Mariola is grateful to all the children who visit her practice daily and to her key teachers: Kiiko Matsumoto (Japanese Acupuncture), Manohar Croke and Dr. Akhila Bourne (Dr. Peter Mandel's Colorpuncture™), Dr. Paul Dennison and Gail Dennison (Brain Gym®), Dr. Svetlana Masgutova (MNRI-Reflex Integration), Dr. Donna Carey (Acutonics®), Dr. Gary Young (Young Living Essential Oils) and many, many others. What manifests in her work is guided by the spirit of Drs. Janusz Korczak, Rudolf Steiner and Georg Kuhlewind.

Contact Mariola:
Telephone: 845-425-7243 (New York) or 413-358-1155 (Massachusetts)
Email: shiningmtnny@aol.com or shiningmtnma@aol.com.

Index

Notes